piano music repertoires

YUMI SAIKI

"JOY"
for piano

斉木 由美

《歓(かん)/JOY》
ピアノのための

zen-on music

JOY for Piano

This work was written in celebration of the Japanese artist Toko Shinoda who turned a hundred in 2013, and moreover was inspired by her painting on a folding screen of the same title.

The work expresses elemental human joy, which is represented by bright vermilion, and uses sound elements such as consonant sonorities, ascending figures, simple rhythms and percussive writing which derives from the powerful impression of Toko Shinoda's paintings.

Commissioned by the Gifu Collection of Modern Arts Foundation, the work was premiered by pianist Kaori Ohsuga in the concert of my chamber music "Eternity and the Moment" at the museum in 2014. Prior to this concert, the museum held a special exhibition of Toko's works entitled "Listening to Toko – Resonance" and I wrote a short essay to accompany her painting "Joy", which will serve as a guide to this composition.

Vivid Vermillion.

Within blazing and impressive vermillion, no shadow or sorrow can be found.
Vermillion, containing a penetrating brightness and warmth above the glorious silver leaf,
shines brightly.
The large surface that ascends rightwards seems to bring out the elation of joy.

The thick parallel lines create "time", and by layering "time" both vertically and horizontally,
an in-depth "expression" is produced.
The gesture of this "expression" is painted without hesitation, disruption or division,
in a simple and bold manner using the whole surface.

I love the instinct, resoluteness, and the powerful energy.
Vermillion shows the expression of potential or elemental "joy" that makes us humans.

Yumi SAIKI
(Translated by Nahoko Gotoh)

歓／JOY　ピアノのための

　「歓／JOY」は、2013年に100歳を迎えられた日本の美術家・篠田桃紅氏への祝意とともに、氏の同名タイトルによる屏風作品「歓」に着想を得て書いた作品である。協和的な響きや上行する音型、単純なリズムや打楽器的書法など、桃紅氏の作品が放つ力強い印象に導かれた音素材によって、輝く赤に象徴される人間の根源的な歓びを表現した。岐阜現代美術財団の委嘱により、2014年同美術館で行われた「永劫と一瞬〜斉木由美室内楽作品展」において、大須賀かおり氏によって初演されたが、演奏会前に開催された企画展「桃紅を聴く-RESONANCE-共鳴」で展示された同作品に寄せて書かせていただいた散文がそのまま作曲の道標となっている。

鮮烈な＜朱＞

目映ゆいばかりの　印象的な朱の内に　翳りや憂いを見いだすことはできない
朱は　神々しい銀箔の上に突き抜けたような明るさと温かみを孕み　輝きを放っている
右肩上がりの大らかな面は　歓びの高揚感を醸し出しているかのようだ

太い線の並列は「時」を形創り　その「時」を縦横に重ね合わせることで
奥行きある「表情」が生み出される
その「表情」の身振りは　ためらうことなく　中断することなく　分割されることなく
シンプルに　大胆に　画面いっぱいに描かれる

直感と潔さ　強いエネルギーが好きだ
＜朱＞は　人が人であるが故の　潜在的な　あるいは原始的な「歓」の表情を物語っている

　　　斉木由美

Commissioned by Gifu Collection of Modern Arts Foundation
The world premiere：
    May 17, 2014 at Gifu Collection of Modern Arts／NBK CONCERT HALL
    Kaori Ohsuga（Piano）
Duration: approximately 10 minutes 30 seconds
CD：ALM-RECORDS（ALCD-105）

委嘱：岐阜現代美術財団
初演：2014年5月17日、岐阜現代美術館／NBKコンサートホール
    大須賀かおり（ピアノ）
演奏時間：約10分30秒
CD：ALM-RECORDS（ALCD-105）

JOY
for Piano

Yumi SAIKI

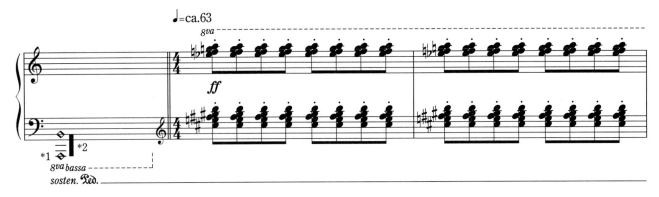

*1 ◇ = silent keys
*2 ■ = cluster

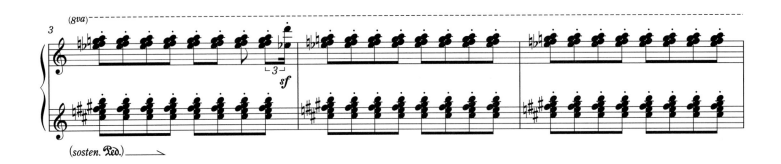

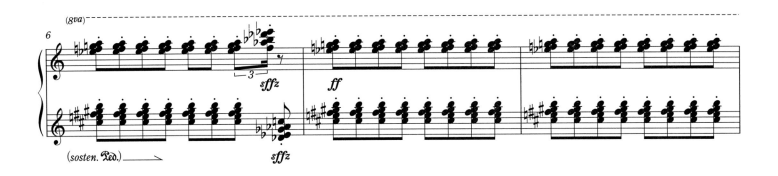

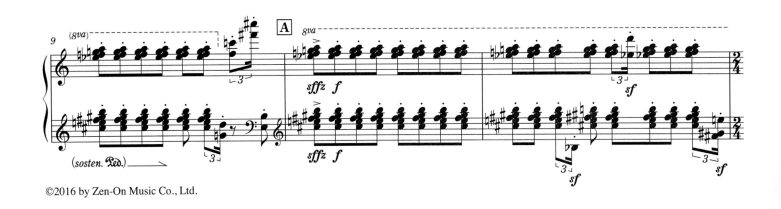

©2016 by Zen-On Music Co., Ltd.

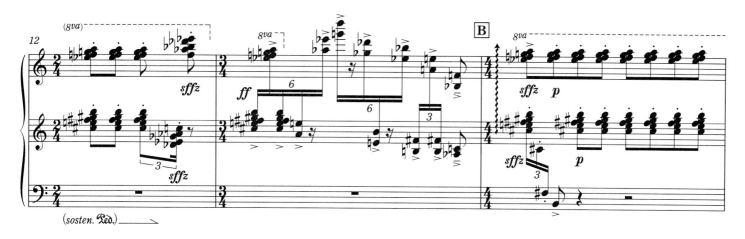
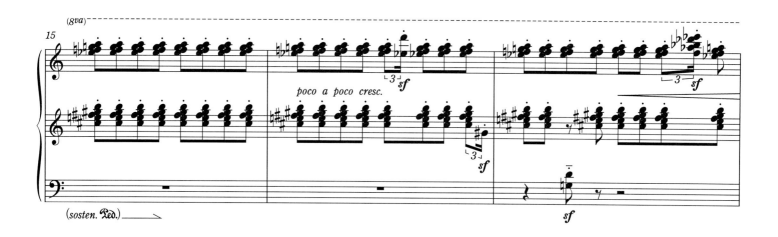

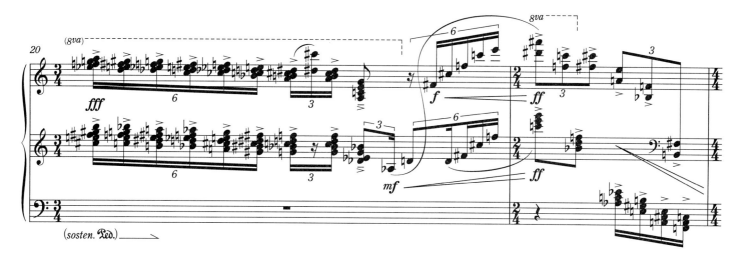

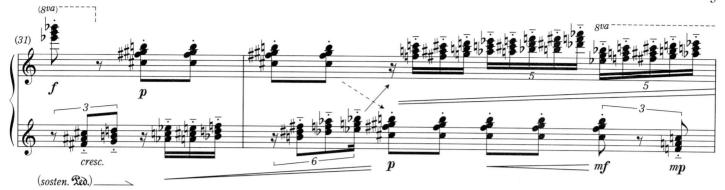
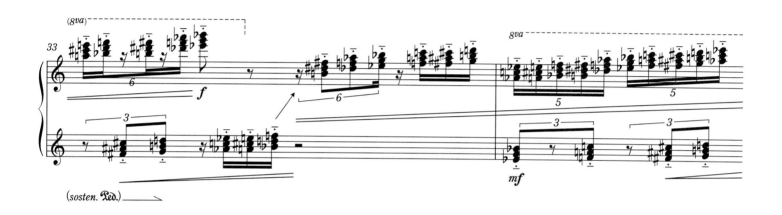
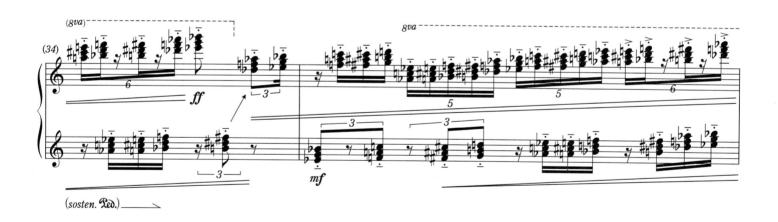
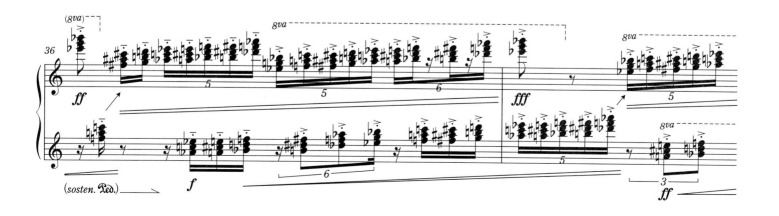

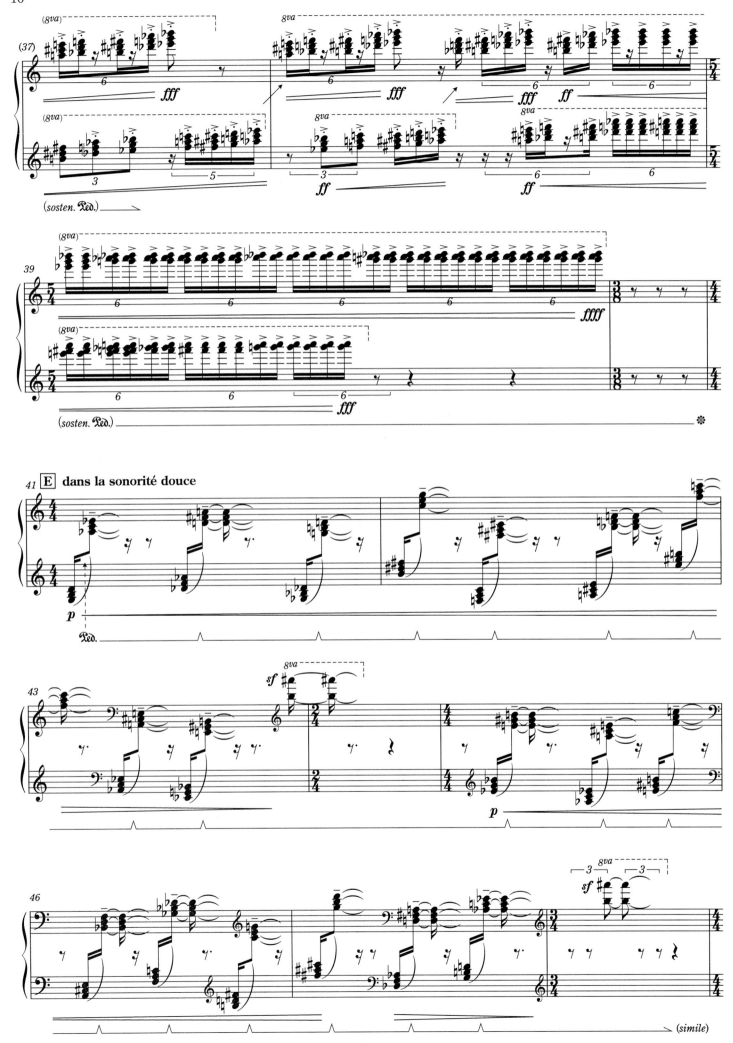

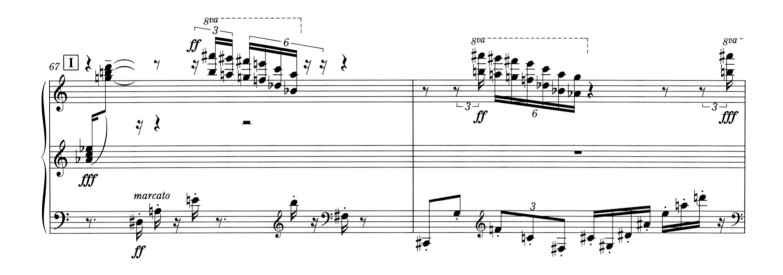
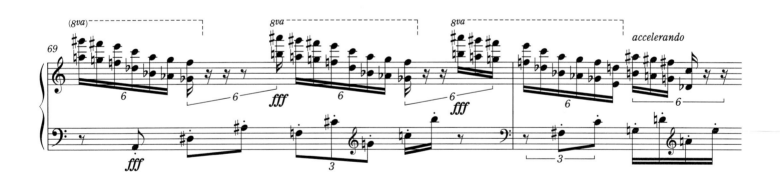
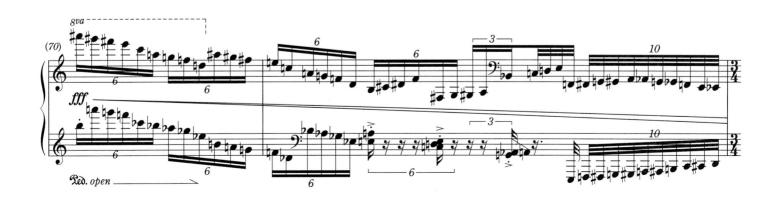

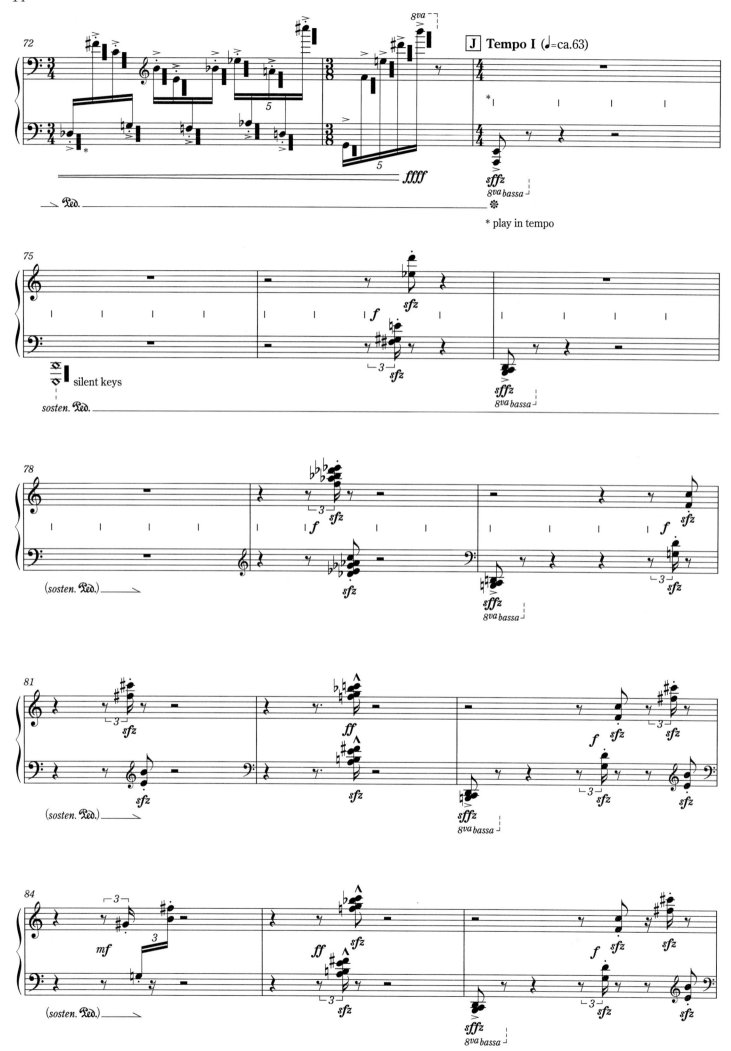

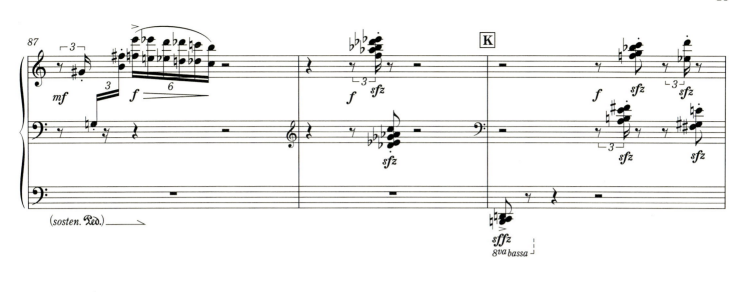

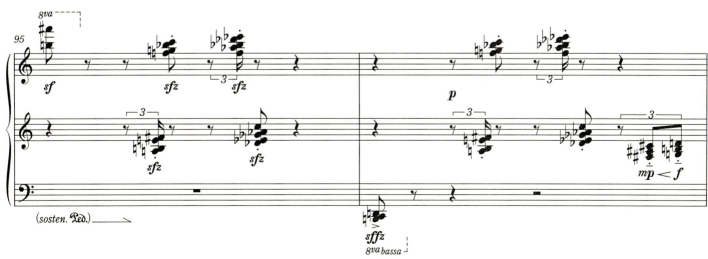

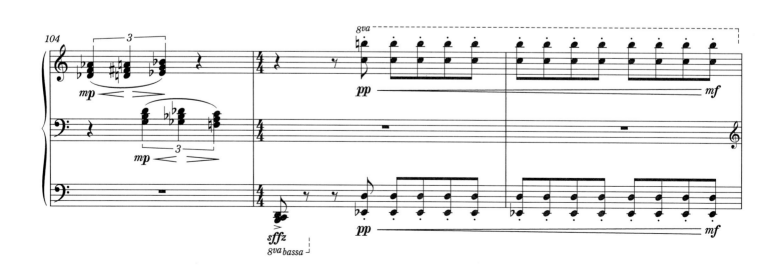

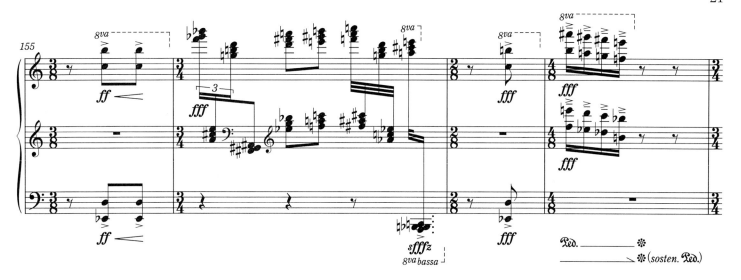
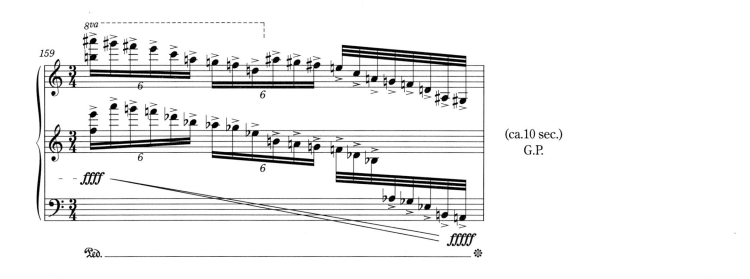
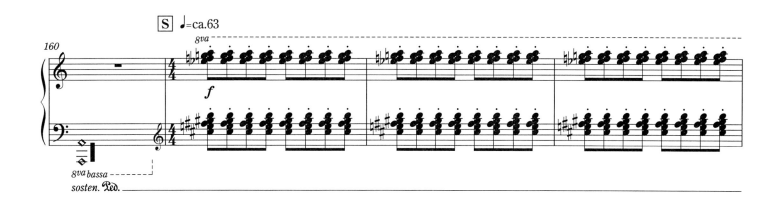
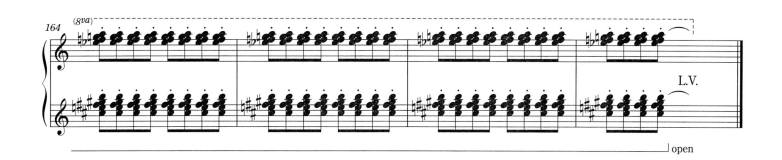

斉木由美：歓／JOY ピアノのための	●
作曲	斉木由美
第1版第1刷発行	2016年8月15日
発行	株式会社全音楽譜出版社
	東京都新宿区上落合2丁目13番3号 〒161-0034
	TEL・営業部 03・3227-6270
	出版部 03・3227-6280
	URL http://www.zen-on.co.jp/
	ISBN978-4-11-169022-0

複写・複製・転載等厳禁　Printed in Japan

16080124